CARAVAGGIO'S DAGGER

CARAVAGGIO'S DAGGER

A pursuit of right action

Hendrik Slegtenhorst

IGUANA

Copyright © 2013 Hendrik Slegtenhorst
Published by Iguana Books
720 Bathurst Street, Suite 303
Toronto, Ontario, Canada
M5S 2R4

All rights reserved. No part of this publication may be reproduced, stored in a retrieval system or transmitted, in any form or by any means, electronic, mechanical, recording or otherwise (except brief passages for purposes of review) without the prior permission of the author or a licence from The Canadian Copyright Licensing Agency (Access Copyright). For an Access Copyright licence, visit www.accesscopyright.ca or call toll free to 1-800-893-5777.

Publisher: Greg Ioannou
Editor: Meghan Behse
Front cover image: Detail from Caravaggio's *The Beheading of Saint John the Baptist* (1608), St. John's Co-Cathedral of the Knights of Malta altarpiece, www.stjohnscocathedral.com
Front cover design: Jane Awde Goodwin
Author photo: Gloria Steel

Library and Archives Canada Cataloguing in Publication

Slegtenhorst, Hendrik, 1948-, author
    Caravaggio's dagger : a pursuit of right action / Hendrik Slegtenhorst.

Poems.
Issued in print and electronic formats.
ISBN 978-1-77180-015-0 (pbk.).--ISBN 978-1-77180-016-7 (epub).--ISBN 978-1-77180-017-4 (kindle).--ISBN 978-1-77180-018-1 (pdf)

    I. Title.

PS8637.L39C37 2013   C811'.6   C2013-905551-7
                                                        C2013-905552-5

This is an original print edition of *Caravaggio's Dagger*.

For Gloria,

with whom I have wandered hand in hand,

So well for so very long:

— Richard Strauss, *Vier Letzte Lieder,* IV, Clarinet I in B♭

LIST OF POEMS

Taxonomy One

Pyre of the Accidental Butterfly

I	Waterside	2
II	Colonists of Colour	3
III	Forsaken	4
IV	Words of Mass Desolation	5
V	Volumnia	6
VI	Entities of Eternity	7
VII	Truth at Wholesale	8
VIII	The Invasive Ideal	9
IX	The Sixth Estate	10
X	Columbia Street in New Westminster	11
XI	Too Often Not a Dream	12

Taxonomy Two

In the North of the Afternoon

I	Alone/Together	14
II	Visit to the Hospital	15
III	Polarities	16
IV	In the Room Next the Laboratories	17
V	North Sea at Sundown	19
VI	Florestan Displaced	20
VII	Detaching That Which Is Near	24
VIII	Lisle	25
IX	Social Oratory	26
X	In the Laurentians	27
XI	Sacred Catechism	29
XII	Sinfonia Concertante	30
XIII	Self-portraits in Youth	31
XIV	Island Shores	34
XV	North Sea Arioso	35
XVI	Half in Passing	36

Taxonomy Three

At the Widening of the Narrows

I	New Year's Walk East of Jarvis Street	39
II	Preparing to Let Go	40
III	Touring with Charles	41
IV	Unanswerable Quests	42
V	Near Grays Harbor in Washington State	43
VI	Transmutation	44
VII	At the Silver Sands Motel	45
VIII	Almost in Port	47
IX	At the Rainbow in Burns Lake	49
X	Ashes of the Oceanic Sun	50
XI	*Rivière-des-Prairies vue de l'Oasis de Laval*	53
XII	Centrality	54
XIII	Inside Sunlight	55
XIV	Reconsiderations	57

Taxonomy Four

The Waterways of Avalon

I	The Beauty-sleep of Death	59
II	At the Morning of Time	60
III	Precognition	61
IV	Wanderings	62
V	The Seven Singels of Leiden	63
VI	Hejira	64
VII	Without Masks	65
VIII	Soloist Within the Imprints of Time	66
IX	At Krems on the Danube	67
X	At the Barber's	68
XI	Not Open to the Public	70
XII	The Approach to What Is Heard	71
XIII	Zeus at the Asclepieion	72
XIV	Globalization	73
XV	Arriving in Avalon	74

Taxonomy Five
Confluence of the Tributaries

I	At Rest	77
II	The Windward Slopes	78
III	Common Obligation	80
IV	Calm of the Heights	81
V	*Inamorata, Inamorato*	82
VI	August Storm	83
VII	A Consciousness	84
VIII	Never Gone	85
IX	Examination	86
X	Unconditional	87
XI	The Mermaids' Gold	88

Taxonomy Six
Caravaggio's Dagger

I	Bodies of the Soul	90
II	Bluebirds Over	91
III	*Sehnsucht*	92
IV	Incursion	93
V	Within the Ocean Within	94
VI	Recantation	95
VII	Cantata Text Booklet for the Holy Days	96
VIII	Tea with the Widow	98
IX	Children of Elysium	99
X	The Answer Is in Africa	100
XI	Through Need and Gladness	102
XII	Gondolier	103
XIII	Ordinary Radiance	104

— W. A. Mozart, *K. 581*, I

'''Tain't in poetry, is it?' interposed his father.
'No, no,' replied Sam.
'Werry glad to hear it,' said Mr Weller.
'Poetry's unnat'ral; no man ever talked poetry
'cept a beadle on boxin' day, or Warren's blackin',
or Rowland's oil, or some o' them low fellows;
never you let yourself down to talk poetry, my boy.
Begin agin, Sammy.'
— Dickens, *The Pickwick Papers*, XXXIII

Taxonomy One
PYRE OF THE ACCIDENTAL BUTTERFLY

Nur hurtig fort, nur frisch gegraben!
Es währt nicht lang, er kommt herein.
Come, set to work, for time is pressing;
We have not long to dig the grave.

— *Rocco to Leonore,*
in the fortress dungeon near Seville,
in Sonnleithner and Treitschke's adaptation
of Bouilly's libretto, for Beethoven's 1805 opera,
<u>*Fidelio*</u>*, II.i:13*

I

Waterside

The tranquil bay holds the foreign ships at anchor,
Containers filled with the ravages of Spice Islands
And the slaves of sub-continents. At the port the cranes
Winch away the subsoil of cultures, refill the holds
With cargoes of an economy contemptuous that
It is washed with the light of goodness. The traders
Calculate the guavas of exploitation, the unsown seed
Of pomegranates cultivated by creatures made imperfect
Even by theology, the empty stomach and the breaking ache
Of the heart gnawing at itself as sinews snap with hunger.
In the hollow satisfaction of the city that overlooks the ocean,
Nothing now grows, consumption the imported greed of
Buffet gardens surrounded by sun-drenched fantasies.

II

Colonists of Colour

Many came; many wait. Few chose
To remain. The sudden transmigrations
Stall in a malnourishment of sand
At borders abrupt and far from water:
Definitions devoid of stability,
Fragments forced unexploded
Into the land. In the ragged tree glint
The fiery dyes of accidental butterflies,
Wings in decline torn by exterminated
Angels hovering in the ochreous air.

III

Forsaken

Touching his right temple with the stubs
Of what once were three fingers, the shopkeeper
Gripped his words in small, heavy intervals:
'They will never come back. Those days
'When the town band played in the square
'While we walked arm in arm down Main Street.
'When the last Jews were gone, the life that lingered
'Drained from the land. Only its sunshine remains
'As a memory, and those longings, in what for so long
'Were my dreams, will perish with me.'

IV

Words of Mass Desolation

Stride falls short of the shadow of epitome,
Words cowering within a paragraph too heavy
With the present, stylus on wax destined
For transcription to vellum and parchment.

Your movable type remains flesh become
More scroll than codex, heedless
Of the tardy perfections beyond Gutenberg:
For when you cease to speak, can you then compose
The epigram within the umbra of your epitaph?

V

Volumnia

> *Holds her by the hand, silent.*
> *— stage direction,*
> Shakespeare, <u>Coriolanus</u>, *V.iii.182*

The returning soldier once more wordlessly holds
His mother's hand, and the rending calm slowly
Begins to break apart. Those who stand near fall back,
For he cannot let go the hand that fed him, the hand
That bleeds away his life into the surrounding silence.
The stillness of the breeze works itself over the hands
Of mother and son; and he watches her as both their hearts
Break, immobile in an anguish so cruel
Its taste is pure, each no longer able to defeat
The remembrances of victory.

VI

Entities of Eternity

The maggots excavate canals into the eyes,
Tunnels through the interiors of liquefying bowels,
Entities vying for prominence within
The perilous workings of everyday eternity.

Revulsed, ill-defined promises stagger beneath
A sky burdened with improbabilities,
Its rainbow pretty to look at, while,
At ground-level, the wounds bluer and bluer become,
Till the first flesh falls away.

The abrupt quiet of killing uncovers dying survivors
Impaled by war: heaving torsos tortured on the heavy sword,
Or pieces of hand-held flesh flying heavenwards
With new hearts of shrapnel.

VII

Truth at Wholesale

Yesterday evening, I thought I heard the drumming
Of the Hare Krishna in that constant distance they seem to like to occupy.

And again this afternoon, while I walk, I hear the drums and cymbals,
But now from the bay; and when I reach the meadow in the park,
I see the Festival of India pulling in the passers-by
With a shimmer of westernized Indian harmonies,
And marketing that has gone a touch upscale:
Loudspeakers and electronic gizmos in front of tabla and harmonium,
Pizza added to the free feast, nose paint kept to a minimum,
And lovely guests in fine saris moving about enticingly.

VIII

The Invasive Ideal

Victory comes with fresh fears,
Conquest an impermanence crawling with the larvae
Of primitive infestations, wounds where purpled blood
Pools without egress, decomposes the safety of strength.
The future seldom arrives as it must have been.
The risk taken, the relentlessness of change
Mars it as the silence flows away.

The walls explode; flesh escapes;
On the roofs overlooking the clouded
Distances to the snow-tortured mountains, the gun scope
Seeks a subject of murder, seeks a new kill for belief.

IX

The Sixth Estate

The drunkard, orotund as an anus,
Hurls his guts as encumbrances
Of unwashed litter over the sidewalk cement.
The breeze binding extremities—
Obscure clouds stray across the cornea,
Resuscitated by the blunt sensation
Next the numbness of the heart.

Consuming squalor, the collecting sewer
Of blackened hands turns coins dark,
Opens coffers the melancholy of perfumes
Cannot stain—the taker's speech gasping for air
As the rains nourish walls of aromatic slimes,
The ooze of delicate poison stupefaction from
The promise of the fountain of youth.

X

Columbia Street in New Westminster

The capital of a century and a half ago languishes,
Ambitions of imperial emulation long ago dismembered;
Its Columbia Street crushed, and shining bleakly
In the fearsome sun. On offer in blocks of dilapidated stores
Are cheap shoes, cheaper jewellery, and bad produce;
Decayed fronts, papered over, pleading for leases for buildings
Not yet filled with the eerie rental emptiness of social services.

At the convenience store by the rapid transit station, Vikram,
Identified by his standard-issue name tag, remains polite
And pleasant, an incomplete assimilation from India.
At the sidewalk tables at Starbuck's, young gatherings
Curse loudly, the nearby diners bawling with too much drink.
Muscle trucks, gleaming silver and fat, rumble along
The half-deserted street, cars mutating to junk plod noisily
Across lanes. Several taxis dance into the sunlight. Even as,
In uneven parallel to the capital, the Fraser River coruscates in
Spaces of brilliance that dart across the well-worn glint of train tracks.

XI

Too Often Not a Dream

The sidewalks are smeared with blood. The regal palace
Across the river: pulverized after the rockets fell.
Bewildered inhabitants clog the streets,
Obstruct the soldiers, their guns raised skyward,
Looking for the new Napoleon. From skyscrapers
Workers stare disbelievingly through cracking glass;
From the roofs of buildings, clerks and waitresses
Point to the dust climbing from the obliteration
Of the government, wait for fighter jets to combat
The unmarked planes in the distance. And over
The new wasteland littered with deposits of death,
Charred energy lies hideous as chunks of flesh,
Rose red, the scented petals of their lives, falling.

Taxonomy Two
IN THE NORTH OF THE AFTERNOON

*Des cieux la coupole infinie
Laisse pleuvoir mille feux éclatants.*
The immense dome of heaven
pours down a glittering rain of light.

*— Faust,
alone at sunrise in the fields of the plains of Hungary,
in Hector Berlioz's libretto to his 1846 légende dramatique,
<u>La Damnation de Faust</u>, I.i*

I

Alone/Together

Come a cold autumn
     when the stones
Lie buried in the ground
And the fears have left
     with your uncradled graves.

Come a cold autumn
     when the nights are long and fine
      drawn like cold filaments over snapped bones
  I will take you down then,
  the thin minstrelsy wordless,
  to the emasculated Alexandria
        of my dreams
        and slender hours
     among the intaglio of time.

Come a cold autumn
     we shall carry wet swords
     in a night of shivering locusts
     bring needles against our spines
     and tap vitality as a vein of ice
   dancing
     the perfect vertigo.

II

Visit to the Hospital

Montreal, 1969

Something moves among the manikins
As the sky breaks towards lavender
And people in pastel become ornamental,
Nunnery casements set wide open,
Birdsong counterpoint to the murmurs
And emissions of private property.

Along Côte-des-Neiges the iron fences
Of the reservoir impale skins of lawn
And breeze; light strikes Venetian blinds,
Trickles of night displacing the asphalt sunset,
As the eighteenth floor sees the fog lift,
And the river reappear, intact with the harbour
And bridges of the supreme city of mauve.

III

Polarities

The billows lash at stones, sinking
As mysterious sunsets moving
Ínto a meniscus of desire, carnal
Silhouettes' hands of flame
Clenching the fires that glide
On the flood's liquid quivering.

As the wind stuns limbs and pauses,
Your eyes recall swallows caught in snow,
And our laughter falls away from
Our hunger and expectations—
Your eyes só blue becoming the dístant sea
That drifts over riverbeds feathered with ice,
Longings gathered by parasites,
Gentle beings beneath alien skies
Once ago splendid.

IV

In the Room Next the Laboratories

**Institut de médecine et de chirurgie expérimentales,
Université de Montréal, 1968**

1

After the ceremony we returned to our desks
And dreamed of sunken logs and shores overrun with rushes,
The public address system gutting our ears
While trees swayed in the glistening winds
And rivers searched for the open sea.
In a surfeit of sarcophagi and icons
We continued to exude the fragrance of artificial flowers,
Scan files damp on windowsills,
Aged by traditional rains of emotions,
Posthumous havens of purity.

2

The horizon glows in a haze of heat
Poured upon temples splendid with blemished time:
The desiccated ruins
Dissolving through the ochre sunlight
Deadened to edify the aimlessness,
Disrupting visions intrepid
As seasons of assault.

3

The halls are well walked upon where hangs
The portraiture, exhumations for a moment
To pore over. Eyes gaze as exiles lost
To a heritage struck away, extirpation
Bloodless as the depth of the coming night.
Irises shudder waxenly, and pools of light
Evaporate as switches topple, leaving blinds as eyelids
And corpses as glass.

4

Far in the vista stands a stone wall, gouged
By gateways and stranded light—
In lands of closed eyes rainbows flourish
And green fields are more real than
Allegories of gold, there where there is no
Breaking of the light
And voices are displaced by birdsong.

V

North Sea at Sundown

The breakers shrink, become calmer,
The inflow and outflow darker on the sand;
The beach huts and umbrellas collected;
The wind more subdued
In the hollows of the dunes.

The long beach at Noordwijk
Is almost deserted; two or three
Small groups with flashlights
Spread a little supper on blankets;
Overhead, incoming seagulls.

We sit down near the low seawall
At the edge of the dunes;
Over the horizon, the skim
Of ocean mists turns
The spot of amber sun
Pink and indistinct.

The ocean ripples greyly towards shore,
The far-off surf a translucent green
Until the breaking rays
Are dissolved in the coastal dusk.

Droplets begin to permeate
The grains of sand; the sound of the sea
Growing more deep and steady
As we sit closer together.

VI

Florestan Displaced

Notre-Dame-de-Grâce, Montréal, 1968

> *Ich glaube, es ist schon lange her, dass er gefangen ist?*
> He's been imprisoned there a long time, hasn't he?
> — Leonora, <u>Fidelio</u>, Act I.i

1

This first
August Sunday morning,
Its sunlight clear
And wind fresh,
Has glazed the city's
Metal and stone.
On the apartment lawn,
Children play;
Churchgoers stroll,
Buy weekend newspapers
At the corner store.

Late summer is in blossom,
The city parks and gardens
Dense with grass; a vicinity

Of shifting leaves,
The trees eminent.
In the distance,
The St. Lawrence is visible,
A slight mist over its shores.
Families begin walks,
Windows left open to let in
The slow streams of air
From the pale blue skies
And the river that flows by the island.

2

At times
There is no resolution:
World too exasperating
To be real, and yet,
From the most livid places
Echo the cold spasms,
Pale ruptures of perception:
Opaque and oblique,
The abrupt tides and phosphorescence
Of subterranean seas.

The mire drifts; detritus
Disgorging from a wilderness
Of deltas: a congestion

Of revolutionary débris,
And guttering alleluias,
Adjuncts to drainages emetic.

Steadfast
A silence of renaissance:
An embalmed worship
Isolated in pools of inertia,
The rainless ether of genetic atolls
And sedimentary villages,
Apostles fragrances of design.

3

Stone enigmas,
And the trees high,
Litanies cast from dawns
Of archaic sunrise,
The resonance of colonnades
In which eyes find articulation as
Silver reliquaries.

The breeze ranges the lower city,
And drifts on terraced mountainside,
Blown ashes in summer grottos,
And fissures in a pendulous mist;
The distant Laurentians age,
Septic beneath withering alchemies,

Refraction a memory of limbs
In a quiet arcane,
The clear shimmer of lake-water.

Acidly, the rhythms break,
The damp from congealed autopsies
Fanned out into corridors,
My hands and the cigarette smoke
Motionless among the viscera,
And numb with desires and sleep.

Past the drapes, an enclave of road
And the broken intestines of night,
A dismembered darkness which elapses
Scourged by transfiguration.

VII

Detaching That Which Is Near

Torn on the coin's rim, bleeding
Into a baptism of abstract debts,
My father was an artist
Before the war.
                        In genealogies
Of yesterdays, oceans more wind-blown
Than legendary, my mother still dreams
Of hungry winters.
                        The gaunt airs
That sound distantly, memory's
Baroque resonance, and by a lake of squalls
My friend fatherless.
                        Singing
The heart knew once without words,
My friend motherless amidst the atrophy
Of histories.
                        The days alternate, wait
For returns too fine, and you my wife
Travel over seas of time
In chambers pilfered from darkness.

VIII

Lisle

> *Des seins! des seins!*
> *— an interested observer*

With your amphetamined perplexities
And spermicidal junkets,
Your ionospheres veer
Like shaky resurrections,
Your breasts a graphology of kisses.

Vexed scorpions speak of Beethoven,
The long autumn night
A tropical catastrophe of desire,
Stilled with fjords ornate with pack-ice.

IX

Social Oratory

Counting innocence a blessing, to us
He came, quite lost in belief, and took
Full advantage, sophism unbuttoned and
Conveniently categorical. He spoke
For each and every ideal, the histrionics
Of eclecticism, a charming baroque guilt
That moved with all in tow.

                                        In time,
We spoke no further, preferring to conceal
Bitterness in a pomp of distances, when that at stake
Seemed retribution yet recovery only was.
Created were more remembrances
Destroyed by excisions of pain.
We required visible means of support.
The dark skies and hollow winds
Proved episodic, as we infected the easy waste
That logic denies syllogism to.

X

In the Laurentians

1 Axiom

Afternoon in the early stages of decay:
Another room forming a temporary retreat
From the lake, the light still full, the disorientation
Complete—delusion collapsing under the weight
Of intangibility, shifting from dreams to days.

2 Continuity

The light burns dazzlingly clear,
Sleep a vanishing substitute
For memory, and awareness as calmed
As the lake before sunrise.
Filtering through the eyes
As a certitude of unsure dreams,
The light falls within the iris—
Waves that glisten in the wind
And touch reflected forests, a saturated
Indigo and green allowing perfections
In a substance of sheets of illusion:
Rising towards the light,
The eyelids enclose the dream,
Open the dream, are sure of daylight
And the yellow waters of sun.

3 Enigma

The fragmentation of enigmas
Yields perforated tissues of rising light
That fall into the eyes:
Indecipherable are stratified visions
Of a monochromatic night, calcification
Without reflection—negligent insularities
That deflate in a geology of inorganic time,
Hymnals stained with memories stale
In ellipses of remembrance and oblivion:
Through the clogged hours history
Backs up and drowns itself, the refracted
Residues drawn out by fervent partisans.

XI

Sacred Catechism

Earth paradisial
Forms in the morning's turbid sky,
The wind sounding the leaves, the nearly still
Waters of the lakeshore breaking on emptiness
As, when everything began, angels were moved.

The light strikes the folds of forest,
You from dust creating the wings of the universe
As I blend with the vapours of the evaporating sun.

XII

Sinfonia Concertante

Afterwards, still glowing and wet,
You push yourself up to sit cross-legged
In the middle of the bed to tell me
That someone else, in the same bed,
Had also told you you were warm.
I want to touch your breasts again
As your words sway them towards me.
What became of what we had,
Went – and what was, we squandered –
While as refuge we sought a single phrase
That would not inflict more damage:
The two of us played out
By playing on one another, as if uncertain
Whether the yearning for more
Was simply more farewell.

XIII

Self-portraits in Youth

1 Approach to Middle Night

An arbitrary ritual of ricerars[1]
Constructed on neural channels
Soaked in coffee and chance wines,
The patterns beat dully, steeped
In the smoky asphyxiation of cigarettes.

My senses glisten above a meniscus of breath,
Sounds poured into a calcifying ear,
Atoms to the eye imperfections
Of a parabola of repetition, the careless
Arithmetic held in place by adhesion—
(Must I, then, enter your nakedness
Before recovering ecstasy.)

---

1. Polythematic, solemn music in imitative counterpoint, with extended treatment of each subject.

2 At Midday

Strange retreat—
Into a mythology of avowal,
When gentleness runs ragged and sharply
In estuaries of the mind.

Moreover, the clandestine efforts
Sear with peregrine vengeance—
Coming round sombre corners in the organism,
Unavoidably, I am face to face.

Threadbare resolutions that close ranks
Like disciplined soldiery—
To erode mercilessly in summer storms
Pumping blood in a febrile heart.

Centuries of disavowal
That coalesce in vertical dreams—
Waking remains a point of departure
To cauterize flesh to flesh.

3 In the North of the Afternoon

Irruptions rend the torn mind
And immobile broken ear, smoke
The arterial vortex.

Rainfall in the afternoons of northern cities
Convulses the oscillating intervals that fall into
The allure of error in disjunctions of time,
Spasms of actuality permeated by
The remembrance of waste.

XIV

Island Shores

Evening begins to falter as you light one more cigarette,
Its smoke smelling of the strange beauty of last year,
A slight touch of the fragrance of our first times together.

I ask whó it'll be that you'll borrow from, even as
Our worthlessness wears away the time, the past
Mutilated with indifference.

Incessantly we continue with leaving.

Earlier you wept without derision—though soon after,
In keeping with custom, you felt obliged to retaliate.
Even so, you made a little space to say
You believed in me, and for the first time
Since you went away, I may have
Believed you, even when you say yet again
That yoú're happy now.

But at last the silence supervenes, and for several seemingly
Únending moments, from the windows of this almost
Empty apartment on the nineteenth floor in downtown Montreal,
We look once more, almost touching, to the now dark river
Of our city, night a fragmentary embrace of úntellable light.

XV

North Sea Arioso

Echoes receding under the microscope,
Switching faintly from eye to eye,
The canal's eddying ripplets,
The wind on the surface of the salt
Of the ocean coming inland—
Pinioned by roots and the loss already arisen
In dim seaside dawns.

Between the compromise
And the trains into the cities, much later,
The vivid strip of early sun lingers over the waters,
The coastal lands your eyes,
Images memory thinks it no longer traces—

The medieval graves of the pilgrim church the history
Of orchards, travelling through multiples of desire,
Love raised out of nothing and everything:
Reflections in sunken pastures held safe by the dykes,
The sails of windmills turned by the inland winds
Quickened above the cobblestones of the streets.

Time, and your exterior, burn away.

XVI

Half in Passing

> *My lord, your sorrow was too sore laid on,*
> *Which sixteen winters cannot blow away,*
> *So many summers dry. Scarce any joy*
> *Did ever so long live; no sorrow*
> *But killed itself much sooner.*
>   — Camillo, <u>The Winter's Tale</u>, V.iii.49

1 Early Blossom at Winter's End

I am driving home as the song on the radio
Brings back into focus something of long ago.
The end of winter nears once again, and already
The cherry trees, fleshly ingenuous in unclad
Pink and white, straddle the sun-shot street—
As if bouquets for her I no longer search
To remember; though sometimes revisit, irresistibly,
Despite my resolutions.

2 Unawakened

I dreamt I did not smell of bourbon, or you of rancid sheets
And the wilderness of the city. I dreamt that we were kind,
That you were beautiful, and that your flesh and sweat were sweet.
I dreamt we returned to that place not quite lost that often
We came to, each coupling more and more aware
Of the almost ready return of the almost desired dream.

3 The Perfection of Winter's Remembrance

When you think of me I suppose
It is partly what I may have been
And partly what you think I may
Still be. And I can no longer revive how
I thought you were. Ripeness now gathers images
That glow only with long-held glimmers
Of remembrance—and of recollections
That I would have wanted different.
The gold resided in what once went amongst us,
But what stays is merely the supposed memory
Of the sheen of the lustre it must have had then.

Taxonomy 3
AT THE WIDENING OF THE NARROWS

The beauty of life ... is nothing but this,
that each should act in conformity
with his nature and his business.

— *W. Somerset Maugham,*
citing Fray Luis de León,
<u>*The Summing Up*</u>*, 1938*

I

New Year's Walk East of Jarvis Street

Toronto, 1991

The cold of the first day of the wintering year
Works itself deep into the ends of the fingers,
A northern century's gritty wear displaying itself
On the second-rate brickwork of the street's
Long decrepit buildings, the alien aromas
This year from the Sri Lankan grocery next door to
The East African Agency quoting economical fares
To Nairobi, Lusaka, and Dar-ès-Salaam. Those

Recently moneyed walk the neighbourhood,
Eyeing it for gentrification, while emigrants from
Warmer lands try to weather the winter, bundles
Of rented videos clutched close; the homeless shelter's
Down-and-out form their column to George's BBQ
For this year's free meal of roast chicken; and in
The crowded afternoon of corner bars, cigarettes and
Bottles of beer are rubbed together in simplicities of

Renovated merriness. We walk for some time,
My wife and I, moored in our mobility, thankful
Of each other and our time in the city. The sun
Elaborates the close of the northern day, and the
Brittle rays of light illuminate the city's
Noisy avarice and modest reality—that the
Best of places is for the person, not beyond him;
That the best of times is in the person, not around.

II

Preparing to Let Go

— Mozart, <u>Piano Concerto K. 595</u>, Larghetto

The sun sets, the only colour in a monochrome
Of land and sea and cloud, charting a column
Of yellow upon the rippling bay, as the volume
Of day falters, and gathers itself into the unknown.

The pause abandons the desire to claim,
An utmost joy becoming that sullen opacity
That carries its evanescence of sensation, the requiem
That brings the last and mortal gleam to serenity.

III

Touring with Charles

Kenya, 1989

> *For Charles Kibiru Muraguri,*
> *in the hope he still lives, up-country*

Having polished the exculpatory fool's gold
Of diplomacy and migratory academics,
My wife and I leave behind the embassies
And the consulates and their many rooms to meet in.

While the rest of the van-load still sleeps in its avarice,
Two hundred kilometres west of Nairobi, towards
The land that is his, we descend through six thousand
Feet of ageless openness, on a road built of holes,
To reach the dust-driven floor of the Great Rift Valley.
Giraffes and gazelles sheer off our lines of vision,
The ancient animal's recognition returning
Of the earthbound heart that persists in its beating,
In the opulent and sudden light of Africa.

IV

Unanswerable Quests

The death of my father-in-law, Montréal, 1994

The eastern week of death aches with breath become
Heartbeats of pause, an island wind's gasp
As the sudden sunset strikes orange. Hard granules of snow
Drift and disappear, white in the dark. At the *régie*
We buy wine and brandy. I drink libations to
My captors and liberators; I drink endlessly to myself.
I drink to hear the words I have not lost, exquisite
As those kisses that bitter bring joy.

The obsequies concluded, the same five thousand
Kilometres are flown across a continent.
On Locarno Beach we watch the glaucous waters
Drive to the shore, a soft-sounding foaming
Left at the edge of returns to the sea. The shoals
Are white-capped, and the hard wind is cold. My wife
Takes photographs of the city on the peninsula.
The wind pits and webs the waves as they respire.
Like the North Sea in a child's recollection,
Our quests stay sure ánd unanswerable.

V

Near Grays Harbor in Washington State

The harbour fog rolls through the long streets,
Already noisy with the rhythms of the big rigs,
The westbound highway along the front of the motel,
The eastbound lanes binding its back. Through the greyness
Townsfolk drive to work, the loggers already harvesting
More of the second-growth forest; as the shifts
Change at the twenty-four-hour Safeway, and at
The port, and at the all-night motels, where recollection
Rolls around in tins of beer in refrigerators,
Next to the hair dryer with a night-light in the handle,
And imagines the sounds of the railroad
And the loading of cargo at the export docks
That stopped years ago and left town unwillingly;
History, unlike inhabitants, not needing to linger.

VI

Transmutation

A silvery intelligence, in the quicksilver days
That gilded children form, took quintessence far:
Earth, air, water—in their fire glowed my existence.

Later, enough years into it, enough people—
Former colleagues and associates, I suppose—
Convinced me finally it was too fast; for,
It was said, "A person doesn't really know this place
Till he's been here a while—hard to know it
As the others do." I put aside the notion that trash
Remains trash, no matter how much glitters
The gloss of its amalgams. Immersed in an aqua regia
That dissolved the elixir of inner stillness, I continued
Courteously to think I served the social good,
Until the world closed in with carnivorous zest,
And the career, and my restraint, got me.

Well, frankly, no matter. Better the shining,
Argentine lustre of golden days to best conduct
All that electricity, heating the philosopher's stone
That attracts all things that tend to perfection.
I'm skipping through—putting the noble alloy back together—
A burning stone, darting across the moonlit water.

VII

At the Silver Sands Motel

Florence, not on the Arno, but in Oregon.
We've come for the seacoast,
And David, clad, leans back to greet us.

We ask for a quiet room. We get the one
Above the office, near the road, away from
The ocean—I've stayed in a thousand rooms
Like this: spare, cheap, a cinder-block palace.

Like mechanical devotions too persistent
That irritate the vastness of a cathedral dome
By Brunelleschi, I hear the managers' TV,
Gurgling with constancy. Late in the evening
It goes off; early in the day, it goes on.
People no longer want to understand
Quiet: it oppresses them.

                        All three buildings
Stand empty, tombs uncontemplated
By Michelangelo. We're the only paying guests
And we've come out of season. The manager
Has blond, stringy hair and a worn-out look
Not born of fatigue. On the highway, the cars hurtle past

At speeds unconnected to perception, a slur
Not safe to cross between the forest and the ocean dunes.
The Ponte Vecchio of the new age.

                                       Come morning,
The manager, his hair pulled into a short ponytail, stands
In biker's regalia, by the side door of the office,
With coffee in hand, cigarette between fingers;
His new all-terrain vehicle is parked next to
His old Pontiac that time has tortured lovingly.
The manager and his bearded friend, a portrait
Of wasting middle age, are latter-day Medici
Lacking three centuries of money. They pull
Ornate Harley-Davidsons into the sun
From white, unmarked trailers, indisputably
The local Uffizi and Palazzo Pitti.

I ask about the machines. "Yah," he responds,
"Don't get out to ride much anymore. Might get out
"Before the fog rolls over the dunes. The winds'll pick up."
They want to be on the road, away from the ocean,
Freed as Dantean exiles in shadows of republican noise.

VIII

Almost in Port

Back then, I thought myself crushed by your chastity;
Later, of course, that parameter proved vaguely
Liberating. Odd, how longing invades lust, and then
Contempt allies itself with disaffection. Even your beauty
Lost its illusion, your feckless infidelity inebriated
With yourself, while wanting so much to exude
The convention that your passion had had no equal.

On the island all of us searched for the perimeters
Of our understanding, found ourselves drenched
In the ocean's brine, looked for ways to undress
On the public stage without wilful observation.
You drove too fast too; thought your control impervious
To mischance; thought the intersection was only yours
To turn into. All the accumulations of uncertainty
Distorted the deliberate evasions of what was
Remembered, and never retold the same way twice,
Even to oneself. The dawn rose operatically, within
The fine film of morning moisture that had held
The last exhalations of night together with its scent.

On the mainland, exasperation grew from the humus
Of payment without work, entitlement without asking;
And the calibrated meetings in shore-side coffee shops

Were more backdrop for the sinful melodramas you loved
To elaborate on, than cubicles of concern wanting still
To leave aside the leanings of logic and the leavenings
Of reality with an uncertain price. The casino broke.

The cell phone conversations infiltrated air deadened
With calculated triviality. I had put my money down:
All you wanted were the cards. All you got was another joker.

IX

At the Rainbow in Burns Lake

The roadside forest conceals continuous mountain
Clear-cuts, sheared by loggers amputated by
The corrosion of hope. In town the highway runs
Too close to airless motels, seasonal tradesmen
Smoking in doorways, the end of a too-long day in which
There's nothing else to do. Periodic convoys of locals
Pump underpriced gasoline from an unmarked tank.
Young louts intrinsic to small northern towns
Loiter noisily. Bottle-blonde young women, fattening
After unexpected children, make up rooms the morning after,
Or head out in the truck to shop sullen-faced at the co-op.

X

Ashes of the Oceanic Sun

Of and for my father (1924-2001)

— *J.S. Bach, <u>Cantata 156</u>, Sinfonia*

1 Along False Creek, the Ocean Glittering

When you died the days became
Simultaneously longer and shorter;
The nights deeper or shallow;
The evenings overlong or too fine;
And to my eyes came images that do not exist,
And to my sensations the deceptions of reality.
The permanence of the past breaks away
And I sense I drifted
In the same sea you crossed over
To find more, almost against yourself.

2 Between Cities

The elevators and parking lots become too familiar:
The ones at the hospital in the capital
Almost a continent away. The cold spring

Stares blankly over the half-frozen shield
Of the land that lies on the western bank of the river
That flows south to the St. Lawrence—
Rivers of ashes and times that once were,
In places you once came to, before the decades
That went by and are so strangely better known.

And there are all the streets: the same ones,
Though separated by most of a country
And lives much lived; the one in view of the sea,
Another away from the ocean left behind.

It is the same death that brings us back together,
Once more in pain and sorrow,
And then in the endless landscapes of eternity
Where we will forever still search together.

3 Quarter to Twelve

He died ever so quietly,
As if having waited for someone else
To be with her; as if having waited
For us to arrive. He took one breath,
Like any other of the last voiceless weeks,
And then nothing.

                      Death crossed
From what was to what is, and then gently
Filled the space. My mother

Closed his eyes; we straightened
What had remained of his limbs.

"He's gone," she'd said,
Half looking at us, half looking away,
In that still and new loneliness
Now all around her.

4 Dying

When the windows of the last shop have been shuttered,
And the last matter of business rung up at the close of day,
You will have gathered the undertakings of all yesterdays,
And brought them home where they stay in peace.
There—in the great land sought and new found
After the misfortunes of war, and made more
By the artist whose art was life, and its living.

For as the light fades in the evening over the ocean far away,
So does your life fade forever into you:
No man ever loved better,
And no man ever loved so well.

XI

Rivière-des-Prairies vue de l'Oasis de Laval[1]

le 22 décembre 1993

>*À mon éternellement bien-aimée amie de grâce, Cécile (1916-2004)*
>
>*Casta Diva ... a noi volgi il bel sembiante*
>Chaste déesse ... tournez vers nous votre visage si belle
>— Bellini, <u>Norma</u>, I.iv

Winter's white subdues the landscape, the river
Veneered with solid ice between Île Jésus and Montreal;
A snow-flecked narrowness streams along the northern shore,
Attenuated and agitated by the ceaseless wind.

Seen from the windows of Cécile's apartment,
The frozen river flows into the long distance,
Church spires marking its passage, the afternoon light
Easing tenderly towards the deepening tones
Of the blue evening, the cities beginning
To glisten, the river-ice slowly goldening
As the full moon asserts the monarchy of night.

It rises steadily, till its lucent shaft of serene cold
Falls the length of the tributary—uneasy only
When it slips to its end in the slender channel
Of black water, hungry for the swallowed light
That moves within the royal and perfected vastness.

---

1. Montréal's Back River seen from the residential complex *L'Oasis,* on Place Juge-Desnoyers in Laval

XII

Centrality

The declination
>of days of depression
>into nights' encounter of nuances
Of realizations thought lost in
>too many years of sleeplessness,
>successions of misdirected desires,
>acts of ineffectual obsession—
Wanton guides to independence,
>atriums and ventricles that redden
>with the oxygen of intoxication,
>apprehending
The necessary wants of the heart.

XIII

Inside Sunlight

For Gloria

...life is a sort of debt and payment
— Kahlil Gibran, in a letter to
Nakhli Gibran (March 15, 1908)

1 In Leiden

What you tell me sinks into tidal canals
That dissolve the surge of pure meridians.
The waters wash a sky that burns away,
Yet I want to become you
As solar wind among the flowers.

2 Mystical Stanley Street

The scattered days disperse like talk stubbed out
In ashtrays—specks of dust suppressed agitations
Suspended in the sunlight, the pivots of thoughts in squalls
Frequenting an end that approaches misadventure—
A weariness impelled by mirrored inflections
Of distant movements of the mind; and the sudden duration
Of eye to eye—in a place where the deep clearness
Remains unclear. I come to believe I delude myself
There remains still that time that gives and takes away.

3 At Long Beach near Tofino

The shoreline where the green of the rolling sea
Is its counterpoint; the white beach that dissolves
Within harmonic waters, sounding inside the sound,
Mystery altered by the music that unfastens time—

I had thought I could take you towards the uplands of being,
But discovered it is you who went there long before,
And, all this while, had been waiting there, for me.

XIV

Reconsiderations

Citing the cantatas of Bach,
The musicologist[1] offers
That the power of an art that pays necessity
Can equal
The power of an art that must create:

And so brings back the business
Of that song whose lyric
We tend to avoid—where
The regret one has is: not to have done
What one's impelled to.[2]

And that last reconsideration:
That of adopting—
As Somerset Maugham[3] puts it, summing up—
A course of action we thought was right, though we knew
It could not bring us happiness, ever.

---

1. Jack Westrup, British musicologist, and author of a work on the cantatas of J.S. Bach.
2. As Luc Plamondon, Québécois songwriter, conveys so well in *Le blues du businessman*.
3. In the concluding chapter of *The Summing Up*.

Taxonomy 4
THE WATERWAYS OF AVALON

*Door de wildernis van zijn angst
breekt leven als water naar binnen:
een zee, een springvloed van hoop.*

Through the wilderness of his fear
life breaks inward as water:
a sea, a soaring flood-tide of hope.

— Ed. Hoornik, <u>Het menselijk bestaan</u>
(<u>The Human Existence</u>, *1952*)

I

The Beauty-sleep of Death

The opera of life is more unreal than art,
Its final cadence the beauty-sleep of death,
The redemption that slips into the silence
Where mortality beckons immortality,
Wondering whether love was pure
In a work that fell away perfect,
Or too unsure to bring art to life.

II

At the Morning of Time

Katwijk aan Zee, 1951

Half a century before
The past now vivid, there is only
The young couple cycling on the open road between
The town and the coast, their child in a fender seat,
Inflections of wind and the brine of light
Over swaying fields of yellow tulips,
Over pastures receding into sunshine.

At road's end, luminous dunes sweep to
Swells of waves moving visible air
Over swimmers.

The child watches the falling and rising
Of an ocean whose essence stretches away endlessly.
He wants to be in it, become
Its expanse.

III

Precognition

The wind catapults cosmogonies,
Liturgy that the barrens abandon—
An oasis of the palm,
Glacier of the wolf,
The glide of the anaconda—
Madrigals of raging water
Breaking on intercession drifting
High above apocalypse,
And into the maelstrom's castigation,
While the sun-flecked rivers flow.

IV

Wanderings

> *Farewell till then. I will go lose myself,*
> *And wander up and down to view the city.*
> — Antipholus of Syracuse, <u>The Comedy of Errors</u>, I.ii.30–31

The hand of my mother as we walked along the canal in Leiden;

The rattán chair on the deck of the transatlantic ship,
The thoughts upon my father's face as he looked out to sea;

The wooden seats of the train from Halifax to Ottawa,
The darkness of forests drifting by;

Nearby the Rideau Canal,
The rich, radiant daylight in the upper flat on Argyle Street;

On Somerset Street, the first barber shop my father owned,
All in a glow of greatness:

         the child who nothing knew
Of their sufferings—war, imprisonment, bombardment,
Starvation, occupation, destruction, poverty;
Of the risks they took—a new country, a new culture, a new language.

By this they made my mind full, my actions right. And from this
I have wandered through a country incandescent,
Each new day to be found in the aching exploration of the self.

And for this, this incomparable inheritance, lives
The perpetuity of my gratitude.

V

The Seven Singels of Leiden[1]

In the canals and narrow streets
I persist as a shadow and a memory

Walking up the slope to the bridge
I am dispossessed of duration and substance

Turning into the square, the church
Casts a darkness to dispel my history

The spires outline an indistinct sky
As I focus on the early light

And I trace my way as seven singels
Perpetual with the flow of inland waters

Into this insubstantiality I am conceived
And in these glimpses of reality I cling

As a lingering and a formlessness
I am this existence near and faraway

---

1. A *singel* is a moat round a city. Though similar to a canal, the *singel* was built as a component of fortifications. Those encircling the City of Leiden, in the Dutch province of South Holland, were completed in the 16th century; they are interlocking, navigable, and of fresh water from the Rhine.

VI

Hejira

Mein lieber Freund,
The emperor's ballroom is filled with dancers,
Eighteenth-century Vienna brimming
      with allegrettos,
The harpist plucking melodies
      Above the violins.

Mon cher ami,
The mystery of Damascus hangs
      Like a song in the dry summer air,
While our hands search for canticles
      Somehow reminiscent of
      Troubadours before the Renaissance,
Like an ancient glass harmonica long lost
      In the Dark Ages
Among the mauve twilights
      Embroidered with flutesong.

Nonetheless, my friend,
The great god Pan dances between our memories
      Which spiral underneath trade winds
      Towards the Mediterranean Sea,
While we look for a Phoenician ship
To take our desires to Palestine.

VII

Without Masks

Faces flow
Upon a sole apprehension,
Cluster
In fragments multifarious,
Bleak tenebrosities
In the lustrous dark—

Follow sombre passages
Until are glimpsed the origins
Amid the splendours of oceanic soil and sun,
We and our revelations
Disrobed and dispersed and devastated are—

Each his mortal entity
Upon
The crucifying wretchedness of this earth,
Forever,
World sad with its beauty,
Forever,
Life sad in its beatitude.

VIII

Soloist Within the Imprints of Time

Sunshine lustrous upon the coloured engraving,
Of Viennese buildings alongside the outdoor market—
Translucence the remonstrance of a great chordal splendour,
Beethoven conducting, nearby, in Theater-an-der-Wien.

Much later, the sun rusts away, corroding
The limpid brilliance within the frame baroque:
Resolution altering from ideal to real as exact as
Syllogisms of history that splinter the harmonies
Of shimmering. On April 16, 1819, the composer
Writes to his London agent: "*Notice here that a bar
"Is to be added at the beginning thus*:" the pause,
Clarification; the soloist, in search past incertitude.

IX

At Krems on the Danube

for Paul Morel

The Baroque bells toll
In the pepperpot towers of the parish,
Reverberation ringing
In the resonance of otherworldliness,
The sound of the organ drifting from within,
Vaulted as a half-discerned inner life,
Relinquishing exactions to closer come
To the mortal heart's elemental pulsation.

X

At the Barber's

Over a northern stretch of Toronto's Yonge Street
It's a grey November day; but better weather
Than yesterday, when it rained. Sam Caruso
Stands a metre from his barber's chair, reading the paper.
I take off my jacket and scarf as I say to Sam the weather
Is better than yesterday's. 'Yes,' he says,
'Yesterday it rained so much.'

A black-and-white photograph of two children
Rests on the ledge to the right of Sam's barbering tools.
The photo and its frame have been there a very long time.
So have Sam and his partner Rocky, who, every time I see him,
Is worried: an inflamed mole, a rash on his chest,
Sore gums, a scalp balding too rapidly.

The barber school's gone. There will be no more like Sam,
Who, as always, cuts my hair expertly.
Lather is worked by a brush in a cup—

No fancy heated dispenser like Ernie downtown
Succumbed to. Yet even Sam concedes a bit:
A hair dryer, and perfumed hair spray in aerosol cans.

Always, almost too often afterward, I remember my father,
Working somewhere in the bright space
Between happiness and perseverance.

Saturdays in Ottawa, after the triple matinee
At the Rialto, I'd walk along Bank Street to his barber shop,
And he would cut my hair, always expertly,
And then, oh so many oh too few times,
We would ride the bus home, together.

XI

Not Open to the Public

In museum storage the sacred stone
Is kept in its bitterness, its people's
Disconsolate discontent invisible
Around it. The curators move artifacts
From one shelf to another, categorizing,
Guessing; while by the stone hovers
Destiny's dust, concealing ceremony's
Syntax. Echoes release themselves
When the workers walk away and
Seal the chamber. In unnatural dark
The stone reveals its transformation,
Burns its ancestors as pure abeyance.

XII

The Approach to What Is Heard

After Sibelius: Symphonies Two and Three

In the undulations between lines of sound,
Indistinct recognition brightens along
The small spaces in incompletion, resting
In the rests of silence that speak announcement
Before departure, time held till it impresses
Its expression, moving across the landscape formed
By the waitings of the heart, emptying into the sea.

Far from the flax-blue prairies of exhilaration's
Collapse, and the stone mountains of forsaken
Exploration, over the bottom-land of the delta
Flows the necessity of the river reaching the salt place
Of beginning, there throating the silent awareness
Of the intensity of the surge that seeks not to stop.

XIII

Zeus at the Asclepieion

If time were able to succumb to anesthesia,
It might be saved in that surgery of the ages,
Where physician gods take up the body
And gently place it under the scalpel,
And cut away the lust of durations, to keep
The tenderness that lies unsurely with
The anger of the depths.

And when it awoke, time would be changed,
Itself for a time suspended, and then,
Like the discussions of a dream, it would stand
Away from itself, shaking sleep from
The uncertain repetition of wakening.

XIV

Globalization

We navigate with care, not to shipwreck our voyage
On the somnambulism of Wal-Mart shoppers,
Waggoners who wayfare unwarily
On the aisles strewn with buttery matrons
Gone rancid, mothers with tattoos on their breasts,
Children on the shortening side of discipline,
Men of indeterminate age undefined by baseball caps,
Oversized teenagers who ransack shelves,
Study quarter-pounders, terrorize cell phones,
Unable to perceive when they need to wash.

Laura, the Filipino cashier, wishes us a good day.

At my corner grocer's, Chinese immigrants wage
Another decade's war against wilting produce
And sleep deprivation. No prohibition on cigarettes.
Photographs of family behind the cash register.
Children trained in storefront and storeroom.
Alien accents over the insensible hours and customers'
Unearned entitlements, in order to profit a portion
Of a dollar and a fraction of another day.

XV

Arriving in Avalon

"No point in going," my father said,
"Where everyone else had gone—
"That's how Í came, with you, to Avalon."

Swung through distance and duration
Each of us arrives at those thousand islands
Whose thousand claims beset us—
Each wrapped in continuities and concerns
And connections that will tear and break.
The warm summer has begun its decline
Towards the pungent residues of autumn,
Frozen times broken on realities soon
Too difficult to travel to.

My mother implied in a different language,
"It was the quiet nova of my mind I stepped into,
"The surge of the sounding sea warily approaching
"The faraway shore, all my tomorrows gliding
"As white summer snows against the sun,
"Imperceptible perfections—as are all of you,
"Each who knows me so little so well,
"Each who may have glimpsed
"The shape of my heart and the infinite murmur
"Of my inner self that I am,
"Indivisibly, invisibly inalterable;
"And sung by he who says to me still,

"'And for all of this, I love you,
"'Till and beyond the end.'"

Far away from one another,
We must use the stars to meet again. Over
These uncharted distances of places and times
Falls the dust of starlight, burning us gently
With the longings of recollections and farewell.
Regret becomes the other side of exploration,
And exploration fills with departures, each one
More bittersweet as each bright day makes fade
The colours that once were seen so clearly.
The hearts close by seldom speak,
And the hearts place makes distant
Hold and can hardly bear
All the love that remains more than near.

Taxonomy 5
CONFLUENCE OF THE TRIBUTARIES

zu jener Mitte, die die Zeugung trug....
denn da ist keine Stelle,
die dich nicht sieht. Du mußt dein Leben ändern.
to that dark center where procreation flared....
for here there is no place
that does not see you. You must change your life.

— *Rilke,* <u>Archaïscher Torso Apollos</u>,
a sonnet written in 1908 in Paris
and inspired by the 5th century B.C. torso of a youth from Miletus
in the Salle Archaïque of the Louvre

I

At Rest

— Chopin, Op. 45

He walks embittered beside the North Sea in time's
Careless anachronism, salt tasted in cold rivulets
Of encroaching spray encrusting his northern face.
Throughout dismembered aspirations he trails
The inarguable self he conceives he has lost
As the sea-wind freights its chronicle of recollection,
Forces its collecting brine into thought nocturnal.

The unceasing sound of seaside plays a last
Prelude's unsettled anxiety, its cadenced darkness
Progressions of distance his eyes see but choose
Not to discern. No comprehension obstructs
The acquiescence; no explanation perceptible
While this shoreline treads within himself. More unreal
Than in wakefulness, in reveries he drifts further along
The blackening beach, deeper sleep waiting to warm him,
As the storm closes over and his way disappears.

He walks embittered beside the North Sea in time's

II

The Windward Slopes

> *Mais où sont les neiges d'antan?*
> — *François Villon*, <u>Ballade des dames de temps jadis</u>

1

Snow-sheets, breaking apart into fading fragments
In the last hour before dawn, the headlights
Of the station wagon piercing the pallid darkness
On the highway north. January radio accompanies
The gusting of the whitening wind as it clambers
Through scrub forests guarding great rivers. I drive
Into that other part of the province of the mind,
Into the midst of the snows' sunrise. From October
To May, the northern pureness compresses warmth
Into the splendour of ice. Cedar waxwings and
Evening grosbeaks colour the white palette;
Deer indent the snows; at sunset over river and fields,
The fireplace burns red inside a corona of frost. These
Were the last times that seemed certain. And then
Our aspirations began to rise too much too often
And abilities undiscovered were said to be sure.
Pestilence spread, and contagion melted the snow
That flooded the land and drowned the crops
Left untended, and the farmers let go their industry
To follow the icy rivulets of retreating glaciers,
No more now and then to stand at the blue edge
Of the turquoise lake as the snows begin to fall.

2

In your eyes are the increments of my happiness,
The brown of earth liquid in the light; the warmth
Of morning between us in our cessation of sleep.
Now do the lines of antiquity provide
Yet another understanding in this epic emptiness
That surrounds us; the agriculture of history's
Lessons as it reaps the rotation of crops sown
With seed that could not be recognized. I am
Taught with your tenderness, the touch that moves
Away to return; and on the North Shore mountains
Remains the snow of the heights, like Kilimanjaro
On the plain of our desires, the southern peak
Unblemished by the light. And in the spring when
We return to climb to the snow line we find
Where yesteryear has gone, and melts to return to.

III

Common Obligation

'Take the children,' she said, 'they'll be your comfort.'
So began my long incarceration. On the later journeys
By ship and overland by caravan, the children prevailed
Over every smaller expectation; and the sea and the land
Embittered themselves in the sight of so much wanting.
'Could you not have understood,' she berated, much later,
'That the children are your provenance and your furtherance,
'That they are what we must seek to preserve us for ourselves.'
Nevertheless this inclusion excluded me, even though, much later,
I was emptily happy for it. The children did nothing, however much
Was done for them; and the coming to each place carried with it
Self-destruction and the ravages of want. They would carry
Weapons and kill, and deface the creations of the world.
I longed for what could not be, and sent them at last
By themselves on their way, into the distance of their curse.
'You will always be in their gratitude,' she said, 'and honoured
'As their guide and protector and the one who kept them safe.'
Yet nothing have I heard, however little I would wish it.

IV

Calm of the Heights

Saanich Peninsula, Vancouver Island

Eloquence of the evening elegy
Enriched by hummingbirds, wings
Thrumming as aspirations—fruited paradise
Of the iridescent earth, oceanic breeze
Ascending to bluer kingdoms,
Blurred twilight's invisible cedars
Lingering beneath the beating of wings.

V

Inamorata, Inamorato

A seam of broken ore, exposed
By the fault of mortal geology,
Defines your derivative of passion.
Don't misconceive the incapacities
Of your loveliness, for it evokes only
Turmoil lacking the purposes of desire.
Though your locus of attraction lures itself
To a design of illusion, your love leaves
No other enemy but commemoration.
When moment joins intensity, it breaks apart.
Necessity's insistence makes naked
The unguided best of us, making mistake
The superfluity of intention, willingly bound
In the golden garden of the flesh.

VI

August Storm

Saturating the parched ground of perception,
The summer rain drowns every arid
Disappearance, like voluptuary embraces,

Depreciating in their impatience for reunion.
Hands on the moist hips of the drying morning,
Optimism broken upon the voracious sunshine,

The tremulous mirroring of the gliding rain, memories
Seeking to cleanse themselves as they wash away,
Dancing their dirge in the shallows of the water.

VII

A Consciousness

Time loads too much behind, evades problems
I once could defy. I am less convinced now,
Carcass fraying, my sleep in decay,
Invulnerability obstinately gone.

Yet why can I not reach that place
I do not clearly comprehend nor can describe,
But know I need to reach,
And its truth that waits for me still?

VIII

Never Gone

Mort de Cécile, le 28 juillet 2004

That time was struck from the living, saddened by she
Who died, who lives in the melancholy of infinity.
The past and its places drop away, glaciers
Calving into the sea to drift to disappearance in
The anonymity of the depths; where creatures
Lose themselves when the silent tempest of time
Overwhelms awareness; where the motion of matter
Comes to rest when the stillness cedes to cessation,
Returned to that place of fidelity that cannot be recalled.

IX

Examination

Expressionless, another daybreak erases
The commentaries of the watcher.

Years accumulate: the strength of time
Yielding to its constancy, recollections
Wandering along its pathways
As each arrival of the new day brings
A prevailing bitterness of the sweetness
That may have been, halting the beating of the heart
Another fraction too much and too soon.

Things went on. Once in a while
It seemed like progress, sometimes good luck;
In grander moments, a kind of entitlement;
In humbler ones, something that was earned,
And the supplementary arrogance
With which to admire it all.

Pitiless under the falling of the dry rain of contempt,
Small seconds creep on, and the sentence is time.

X

Unconditional

That we could find what we came together for
        Would be a discovery in a destination
        Where the wildflower meadows
        Of cinquefoil and gentian and moss campion
        Court the rain, and the evening rainbow shimmers
        Longer than the sunlight of sunset,
        And the moon stays silver
In the dreams of the indigo sky. And I will wish
That our inexplicable journey will take us
        Together through the high valleys of the mountains
        To the far-reaching ridges that blend
        Into the nearing horizon, and where I will wish
Our hearts that imponderable joy
        Immeasurable in the unknowable place
        We have found ourselves to have come upon,
        And that so fills the alpine passes
That even the wind winds around as it blows,
The greatening sky arcing above the golden world.

XI

The Mermaids' Gold

Another year's money slips away. The artist
Takes stock of his decline, concludes he's not
At his best in business. There may be profit
In paradise, but the rent needs paying.
He considers his options; reviews the balance sheet
Of his personality, the twine of time running on,
The calipers of consciousness closing closer,
Measurements fewer but more mortal each day.
His operatic existence sings to a libretto
Logic has abandoned, yet accumulates dramatic flaws
Of that vital power through which his music enters
The astral dominions of other worlds, even into those
He cannot hear or be sure he has found.

Taxonomy 6
CARAVAGGIO'S DAGGER

Die Zeit ist ein sonderbar Ding.
Wenn man so hinlebt, ist sie rein gar nichts.
Aber dann auf einmal, da spürt man nichts als sie.
Sie ist um uns herum, sie ist auch in uns drinnen . . . .

Time is a strange thing.
When we live from day to day, time means nothing.
But, then, suddenly, all we feel is time.
It's around us—it's inside us . . . .
— Marschallin, <u>Der Rosenkavalier</u>, I

I

Bodies of the Soul

'Excoriate me,' complained the mystic.
'Flay my flesh till I fall away into the fatal kingdom.'
The Swiss mercenaries obliged him. It was a sunny day,
And they attended to him slowly and with care. And in the piazza
The audience appreciated the refinement of the soldiers' technique,
Even a bit more than all the other penitents in their eviscerated ardours.
In due course, when his eyes were gouged, the mystic trembled with ecstasy;
And, late in the afternoon, as he sensed expiration, he merged
With the agonies of the others as one more of the countless
Ribbons of red with rivulets that sprang to dry in the summer heat.

When thirsty, the experienced executioners had demanded young wine,
And when they drank from the cups the sparkling carmine bubbles
Broke beneath their breath. The mystic had whispered
In a translucent voice that he felt that his consummation
Soon would come; but already by this moment the crowd
Had thinned, a little bored with the butchery; beginning
To look forward to the evening meal and the cooling breezes
That accompanied the receding of day; and the vendors almost at
The same instant began to hawk their wares more hoarsely,
For though the piazza had overflowed, business had been slow.

II

Bluebirds Over

Sweating into stone by fear, dripping
From above, coming by sea, softly piercing
Intestines, armaments petrifying the kingdom,

Fragmentation of fracturing metal
The flesh of the senses.

Memory evades memory,
Distills remembrance
In the passage of wordlessness over the tongue,

Veracity looks out over in
The face of compounding time. Below,
The linnets' singing on the cliffs, of the coming of the waves.

III

Sehnsucht

Longing now rises: mystic potion reddening
Blood in the snow-clad desert, sky imbued
In equatorial winds coursing to the swollen ocean:
Yearning's desire
           Body lashed across
The unrigged mast as it breaks into life without death,
The sand of the sirocco flailing the waves
Sinking beneath the emptiness of splendour:
Yearn in desire
           While golden rains transfigure the unseen,
The coastline thirsts for erosion; being, half dissolved,
Returned to the ocean deep where the still light
Restrains itself not to reward its extinguishing;
And, in the colourless heart of perpetual drowning:
Yearns for desire.

IV

Incursion

Satisfied by the art of mutilation and his pound
Of living flesh, the soldier dangles the wet blade
From his hand, as his troops pitch the bleeding corpse
Over the embankment into the flow of the river.

The dead bulk bobbles downstream between waterfowl,
Red quickening the green water; till, their actions diluted,
Their desires replenished, the infantry departs.

On the far bank of the river, scorched faces changeless
On the unchanging shore, the women and children
Watch the soldiers move on, the land ripe with sun
And split with heat, grass as grey as the mute midst of day.

And in the distance the horses run, shapes obscured
By the dust raised by the hooves of the galloping herd.

Hemmed in by rough waters and the sun-battered
Cliffs on which dust-covered men now appear,
The horses race towards rockfall in the gorge
Through which the rapid river plunges. They clamber
Loudly over the stones, begin to break legs.

V

Within the Ocean Within

Waist-deep and naked in the brittle sea,
He looks out to the horizon beyond the waves
As it falls away on the other side of the world.
The waters undulate against his elbows,
Break away the flakes of skin dried by
The cold of the sun. The brine laps against his belly,
Seasons the hair of his body with ancient
Deposits of the salted spice of the seas. He seeks
To remember what he was when upon
The other turn of the curve, what he is
When he turned to this. The light from the star
Disappears dissolved into the depths of the blue.
The water procreates him, pulls him away.

In this oceanic finitude sparkles the light of life
And its failing knowledge; but the beauty is so great
That still it stirs the cold of the organism
That only half-sees and feels only half.

There is no leaving.

VI

Recantation

When I broke your hands and burned your body
At the stake, I found a happiness within us
That no search for liberation had found: not in
The countryside marshes where we lay till sickness
Found us, and not on the castle towers where we
Looked upon the bewildered sea, our arms clasped
Around each other to steady our standing against
The high assault of the storm at its landfall. Now
The smell of the kindling is sweet, and the fardels
Crackle as the ice that breaks from the houses
At the coming of spring. Your body writhes
To escape the cold, and your fingers twitch beneath
Your motionless wrists. You look at me with
A fierce sadness, the light inside your soul flaming
Large before it fades to exhaustion and is consumed.
I remember this now even today in the years gone by,
And revere your supplication. As you fell away
Portion by portion, more open than the heavens of time,
I saw how the heat of our common intensity
Charred the bones of our belief, and left you standing
Till the stake surrendered and collapsed. So unlike you
When you touched the wellspring of my soul by
The brushing of your fingertips against my cheek.
I almost wept then, but now I think more of your
Ascension into the smoky firmament, while I dwell
Here reckless of my actions, certain that extinction
Fires the mind and brings everlasting torment.

VII

Cantata Text Booklet for the Holy Days

1 Parallel Chaconne

> *sei jetzt doch, o Gott, mein Hort*
> be now yet, O God, my sure retreat
> — *Johann Rist, in <u>J.S. Bach</u>, Cantata 78*

The hard bargain, its shrewd handshake
In the marketplace; the passacaglia mysticism,
Layers above and amongst: simultaneous
Dichotomy and combination. The statue of the saint
Sustained by alms; temples of money encroaching upon
Ionic columns and vaulted ceilings and histories
That reach for omnipotence. Monteverdi
In San Marco. Rothschild at the Bourse.
Michelangelo commissioned; Caravaggio with the dagger.

The antipodes of knowledge seek one another,
Carrying upon and between them the ceaseless burden
Of the fire-wrought soul half-wrung from sacraments.

2 Hidden by Sight

> *O Seelenparadies, das Gottes Geist durchwehet,*
> *der bei der Schöpfung blies....*
> O paradise of the soul, through which God's spirit blows,
> which blew at the Creation....
> — Salomo Franck, in J.S. Bach, <u>Cantata 172</u>

In paradise the late winter snows fall
As silences behind sacred chorales, theology
Breaking away, wanting self-containment,
Wanting more than incomplete enclosure.
It is the sound unheard that compels most constantly:
Can be divined but not quite understood: can be sung but not
Quite said. It dwells in the human counterpoint:
Unpromising fugal themes repeated almost improbably
Until the whole seems apparent just as
It starts to shift again, modulating beyond
The nexus of integrity, to come, once again,
Upon the complications of disintegration—
In each flake of falling snow, differing in
The white obscuration that congregates to come
To its place from places unseen.

VIII

Tea with the Widow

Berlin, 1976

Frau Quast nicht gewidmet

In old Berlin, Frau Quast invites us to evening tea,
In the parlour of her bullet-riddled *pension*,
Its brocades as heavy as selective memories,
Yellowed light as wan as the hunger
For what might have been. Frau Quast brings out
Her photo album, thickened with the brown of years.
'*Mein Mann, ja, was in unser Wehrmacht*; he fought bravely,
'Against the invaders. Yes, a good person.' Many photographs
Are missing. 'The Americans tore out all the pictures of Hitler.
'My husband drove him personally, right here, nearby.
'He died, in exhaustion, already many years ago. With
'No war, without the armies he would be an old man.'

She pulls the greying cerise shawl round her shoulders,
Stares unhappily at the cold teapot, wonders aloud if we have
American money; then complains about the divided city;
Says bleakly she'd have liked to live better.
She looks lost and too intently quizzical when she asks us
Why she would have deserved what her life has come to.
'Things,' she states flatly, 'were not that bad.'

IX

Children of Elysium

Oboes of choric memories:
The cantus firmus that delves through
The fugal overlay: near the outskirts of the northern city,
Near woods yet miraculous, mysticism in
A sharpening prelude—

O solitude secret as the stars' constellations,
Silvered hands that displace clear tinctures of melody with
The dissonance of immeasurable distances
Of the onset of recollections,

In the seaside of an October day: Pacific fog
Green-grey over the glitter of water.
Under the evening's merging of blues and yellows,
Moves this interplay, through an earthliness
Transcendental, forgiving and forgiven,
Its being brought within.

X

The Answer Is in Africa

> *Wer meines Speeres / Spitze fürchtet / durchschreite das Feuer nie!*
> He who fears my spear-point shall never pass through the fire.
> — *Wotan,* <u>Die Walküre</u>, *Act III*

Abdalla sells essences of perfume by the sphinx at Giza,
And gold rings in private antechambers; and in Sakara Road
Mohamed offers silk or wool carpets made by hand. Later,
When Fayez has got us up-river to Aswan, from the felucca
We watch the ibis and the floating lavender of water hyacinth.
Sayed, cupping his hands in the river, says,
'If you drink of the Nile, you will always return.'

There is no fragrance in despair; only stench.
The pianist on television speaks startlingly,
Completely involved by the music. Mozart.
Apparently not a single thought given to earth, absorbed entirely
By human nature—brief joys and plangent interactions
In the lightless, glittering byways of the soul overstrewn
With the odours of the soil. In Lusaka market,
Fruit, fish, and flies linger competitively. Our stomachs full,
Black-market kwachas in pocket, we follow the long streets

Dusty with the plumes thrown by passing trucks and feet.
Yesterday, we met the insurgents.
Today, Moyo takes us round by flatbed truck.

In the shops along the muddy streets of Dar-ès-Salaam,
Bright bolts of yellow cloth reflect a sun of gold,
The earthen fragrances elaborated in the answer
That ís in Africa—divinity released in the embrace
That brings existence tó the mágic fire of passion:
We fly into the Zimbabwean dawn rising ochre and orange
As flame over the vast plain.
To dare to do what is loved
Returns one to that darkest place with its clearest light
That blinds so one can see.

XI

Through Need and Gladness

He sees her every day. Both are aging.
The clearness in her brown eyes holds
A subduing compassion where beauty's heart
Abides. He looks at her eyes very often,
For he is in love with her and cannot
Stay away. It is the sole presence
That makes frail his self-sufficiency,
Causes him to put philosophy by, reminds
That art is not the archetype of life.
He wants more for her than he can gain
To give. She is his only greed, his only
Grace, and through her eyes he sees
The unforgotten endlessness of everything
He has yearned for, and everything
He has learned no longer to possess.

XII

Gondolier

The idyl breaks as Venetian glass under the heavy rain,
The idolatry of the ideal broken as the intestines of a night
White with wakening, slivered by indigestible shards
Transparent to the hands laved with the inundations
Of the rising lagoon. Saintly marks identify the oarsman,
His aging gondola on the barcarolle of the canal
Between the aquamarine ululations of the mouths
Of the Po and Piave thirsting for the industry of the depths.
And in this twilight of temperament become brittle
With brine borne in the blood, and veiled by eyelids
Made thin with subcutaneous sight, he studies no more
The broken ornament, takes the tide that takes the tithe
Of time, and looks at the city that sinks away as it ever
Becomes more beautiful with the life it cannot keep.

XIII

Ordinary Radiance

> *... but I shall see*
> *The winged vengeance overtake such children.*
> *— Shakespeare, King Lear, III.vii.65*

A distance almost too far from the armoured personnel carrier
And his companions, the soldier walks along the earthen roadway.
He reveres this landscape of spring meadows, the pale sunshine
Of the dawn upon it, and, as if impelled by longing,
He pauses for a long, lingering while.
It is when he starts to turn back that he spots
Movement in the high grasses near by.
He parts his lips, about to call out,
When the two children scramble onto the road,
And stop. They are smiling. After a sliver of time,
He motions them to approach.
When they reach him, the soldier kicks the boy hard to the ground,
Takes out his knife, drags the girl forward, cuts out her left eye,
Then her right, pauses, pulls up the boy, severs his left eye,
Waits as the boy thrashes, then carves out the right.
With both arms, he shoves the children away.
They are screaming, silently, as they stagger further down the road.
The soldier tosses the boy's right eye in a long arc
Into the distance, where it rolls to a halt gathering bits
Of blossom and soil. He puts the knife in its sheath,
Not wiping away the blood and threads of flesh.
Absent-mindedly, he sweeps his fingertips
Against his uniform. He takes a small breath, automatically

Lights a cigarette from the pack he has pulled from his pocket.
He exhales as he appraises the contortions
Of the girl and the boy in the morning light.
After a very long moment, his attention returns
To the brightening sky, and his freshened thoughts come back
To his several companions and the war to be won.

Krems, Österreich

North Conway, NH
North Truro, MA

Alma, NB
Edmundston, NB
St. Stephen, NB
Seal Cove, Grand Manan, NB
Lac-des-Seize-Îles, QC
Montréal, QC
Gananoque, ON
Ottawa, ON
Toronto, ON
Banff, AB
Edmonton, AB
Bowen Island, BC
Burns Lake, BC
Kelowna, BC
Revelstoke, BC
Saanich, BC

Vancouver, BC
16 July, 2005

Acknowledgements

My thanks to the Canada Council for its 2004 professional writer's grant, which was particularly welcome during the definitive stage of composition of this book.

Some of these poems first appeared (a few in slightly different form) in the following publications:

"At the Silver Sands Motel," *Qwerty* (Fredericton, NB), 29, 16 (2013).
"Colonists of Colour," *Descant* (Toronto, ON), 159, 43/4, 139 (2012).
"Wanderings," *the new quarterly* (Waterloo, ON), 120, 126 (2011).
"At the Morning of Time," *Grain* (Saskatoon, SK), 38/3, 66 (2011).
"Zeus at the Asclepieion," *Grain* (Saskatoon, SK), 38/3, 67 (2011).
"*Rivière-des-Prairies vue de l'Oasis de Laval*," *Prairie Fire* (Winnipeg, MB), 31/2, 98 (2010).
"Common Obligation," *Prairie Fire* (Winnipeg, MB), 31/2, 96 (2010).
"The Answer is in Africa," *WordWorks* (Vancouver, BC), 18 (Summer 2010).
"Too Often Not A Dream," *Contemporary Verse 2* (Winnipeg, MB), 31/1, 40 (2008).
"Touring with Charles," *Contemporary Verse 2* (Winnipeg, MB), 31/1, 41 (2008).
"Gondolier," *Canadian Literature* (Vancouver, BC), 194, 93 (2007).
"In the Laurentians," *Canadian Literature* (Vancouver, BC), 188, 103 (2006).
"Self-portraits in Youth," *Canadian Literature* (Vancouver, BC), 183, 87 (2004).
"Sinfonia Concertante," *The Fiddlehead* (Fredericton, NB), 222, 29 (2004).
"Near Grays Harbor in Washington State," *Descant* (Toronto, ON), 127, 35/4, 225 (2004).
"Self-portraits in Youth," *Canadian Literature* (Vancouver, BC), 181, 60 (2004).
"Ordinary Radiance," *Windsor Review* (Windsor, ON), 36/1, 38 (2003).
"Alone/Together 1," *Colorado Quarterly* (Boulder, CO), 28/3, 46 (1979).
"North Sea at Sundown," *Quarry* (Kingston, ON), 23/3, 16 (1974).
"The Seven Singels of Leiden," *Quarry* (Kingston, ON), 23/3, 15 (1974).
"Hejira," *The Far Point* (Winnipeg, MB), 7&8, 75 (1972/73).
"Tuesday," [published as "Visit to the Hospital"] *Ala* (Buenos Aires), 54, 2 (1971).

Iguana Books
iguanabooks.com

If you enjoyed *Caravaggio's Dagger*...
Look for other books coming soon from Iguana Books! Subscribe to our blog for updates as they happen.

iguanabooks.com/blog/

You can also learn more about Hendrik Slegtenhorst and his upcoming work on his blog.

hendrikslegtenhorst.iguanabooks.com/blog/
www.culturalrites.com

If you're a writer ...
Iguana Books is always looking for great new writers, in every genre. We produce primarily ebooks but, as you can see, we do the occasional print book as well. Visit us at iguanabooks.com to see what Iguana Books has to offer both emerging and established authors.

iguanabooks.com/publishing-with-iguana/

If you're looking for another good book ...
All Iguana Books books are available on our website. We pride ourselves on making sure that every Iguana book is a great read.

iguanabooks.com/bookstore/

Visit our bookstore today and support your favourite author.

www.ingramcontent.com/pod-product-compliance
Lightning Source LLC
LaVergne TN
LVHW051601080426
835510LV00020B/3085